PUPPET PLAY

The Tortoise
and the Hare

Moira Butterfield

Heinemann
LIBRARY

First published in Great Britain in 1998 by Heinemann Library,
Halley Court, Jordan Hill, Oxford, OX2 8EJ,
a division of Reed Educational & Professional Publishing Ltd.
Heinemann is a registered trademark of Reed Educational & Professional Publishing Ltd.

OXFORD FLORENCE PRAGUE MADRID ATHENS
MELBOURNE AUCKLAND KUALA LUMPUR SINGAPORE TOKYO
IBADAN NAIROBI KAMPALA JOHANNESBURG GABORONE
PORTSMOUTH NH CHICAGO MEXICO CITY SAO PAULO

Editor: Alyson Jones
Designer: Joanna Hinton-Malivoire
Illustrator: Jan Lewis
Printed and bound in Italy.

02 01 00 99 98
10 9 8 7 6 5 4 3 2 1

British Library Cataloguing in Publication Data
Butterfield, Moira
The tortoise and the hare - (Puppet play)
1. Tales - Juvenile drama 2. Children's plays, English
3. Puppets - Juvenile literature
I. Title 822.9'14

ISBN 0 431 03480 X (Hardback)
0 431 03484 2 (Paperback)

You will need scissors and craft glue to make
the puppets and props for your play. Always
make sure an adult is there to help you.

CONTENTS

THE STORY OF THE TORTOISE AND THE HARE

The hare likes to rush about. He thinks fast is best, and he laughs at the slow, plodding tortoise. Now you can make some puppets to act out their story and discover how the tortoise surprises the hare!

READING THE PLAY

There are three puppet characters in this play:

The Tortoise
Slow but careful
and reliable

The Hare
Fast, impatient
and boastful

The Crowd
A group of
animals

During the play, the
puppeteer speaks.
That's the person who
works the puppets.

Do this part in an
ordinary voice.

If you want to perform this
story as a puppet show
there are some tips for you
on pages 6-9.

If you like, just read the play
out loud. You could share the
book with a friend and play a
part each.

The play is split up into parts. Next to each part there is a name so you know who should be speaking.

Who cares about being reliable? Fast is best!

Hare

Sometimes there are stage directions. They are suggestions for things you might get your puppets to do.

Put the hare and tortoise on stage together. Shake whichever puppet is talking.

Making Puppets

What you need

* Card
* Paint or coloured
  paper
* Plant sticks
* Scissors
* Pencil and ruler
* Cotton wool
* String
* Glue and sticky tape

1 Draw an egg shape about 11cm high on to card. At the bottom draw two holes 1cm apart, big enough to fit your first two fingers through.

2 Draw your puppets using the egg shape as the body and cut them out.

3 Carefully, cut out the holes so that you can push your fingers right through them.

6

TORTOISE AND HARE DECORATION

Paint the tortoise shell green, and then paint some bold swirls on it, or glue on pieces of string shaped into swirls. Glue some cotton wool on to Hare's ears and tummy.

CROWD

Draw a crowd of animals onto card. Cut them out and tape a stick on to the back. Paint the crowd, keeping the picture simple so your audience can see what it is meant to be.

To work the main characters, push your fingers through the holes to make legs.

Making Props

What you need

* Card and paper
* Silver and gold foil
* Plant sticks
* Scissors
* Black pen and ruler
* Glue and sticky tape

Moon and Sun

Cut a moon and a sun shape, about 10cm across, out of card. Wrap silver foil around the moon and gold foil around the sun. (The best place to find gold foil is around a chocolate bar.) Glue or tape sticks to the back.

Race flag

Cut a rectangle of paper 160mm by 60mm. Colour one side as a black and white checked flag. Then fold it around a stick and glue the edges together.

MAKING A THEATRE

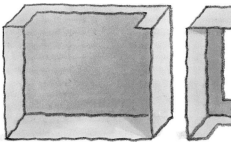 

1 Cut the two bumper packets as shown. Tape back any strips that fall off and tape all the joints to make them secure.

WHAT YOU NEED
* Two bumper-sized cereal packets
* Two medium-sized cereal packets
* Coloured paper or paints
* Glue and tape
* Scissors

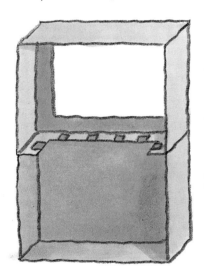

2 Glue the two together as shown and add some tape too, to make the join really strong. Glue and tape a medium-sized box to each side to help your theatre stand up.

3 Decorate the theatre with coloured paper or paints. Stick extra card shapes on if you like, such as a pointed top.

4 Stand the theatre on a table so you can comfortably hide behind it with your puppets and book. Prop the book inside, or lay it flat on the table. Then practise before you invite an audience to watch your play.

THE TORTOISE AND THE HARE

Pop your head up.

Puppeteer

Hello. Here's a question for you. Do you think it's better to be fast or reliable when you do a job? Well, this story will give you the answer.

Duck down and put the hare on stage.

Hare

Hello. I'm Hare and I'm really, really fast. Just look how fast I am!

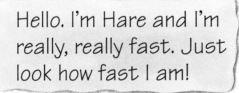

Whizz the hare from one side of the stage to the other. Then put the tortoise up, too.

Put the hare and the tortoise on stage together. Shake whichever puppet is talking.

Hare

Tortoise, you're so slow! A snail could run rings around you!

Tortoise

That may be so – but I'm reliable. In the end I always get where I want to go.

Hare

Who cares about being reliable? Fast is best!

Tortoise

Alright, let's have a running race. We'll see which of us is better.

Shake the hare up and down a lot to show he is laughing loudly.

Ha, ha, ha! A running race! Very funny! Ha, ha, ha!

Hare

Tortoise

I'm serious. We can do it this afternoon, if you like.

Hare

O.K. I'll rush around and tell all our friends to come. It should be a good laugh!

Take off the tortoise and the hare. Pop your head up, along with the crowd prop. Talk to the audience.

Puppeteer

The race is going to start. Cheer, everybody!

Pop back down again. Wiggle the crowd up and down and shout 'Hurrah!' along with the audience. Put Hare up.

Hare

Thank you, thank you. This won't take long, folks. I'll win in no time.

Put the crowd down. Hold the tortoise and the hare up on one side of the stage.

Hare

Ready, steady. Let's go!

Rush Hare across the stage to the other side and off. Move Tortoise very slowly across to the other side and off.

Tortoise

It's important to get a good steady start.

Hold up the cheering crowd and put the hare back onstage, rushing across from the left to the right. When he says he can hop, hop your fingers. When he says he can run backwards, run your fingers backwards.

Hare

See how fast I can go? I can even do it hopping on one leg.

Wiggle the crowd up and down and cheer.

Hare

Look at me! I can even go fast running backwards!

Take the crowd off the stage so now the hare is alone. Take the hare off one side and bring him back on the other side of the stage, as if he's raced further along.

I'm so far ahead it's boring. There's no competition.

Hare

Put Hare on one side of the stage.

I think I'll sit down and wait for Tortoise. I'll still win easily.

Hare

Hold up the sun prop above the hare's head.

> It's lovely and warm today. It makes me feel quite sleepy.

Hare

Make yawning noises.

> I think I'll have a nap before winning.

Hare

Sit the hare puppet as if he is leaning, fast asleep. Take the sun prop off.

Bring the tortoise on, shuffling across the stage past the hare.

Tortoise

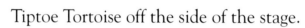

Well, well. Here's Hare and he's fast asleep. He looks so peaceful I won't disturb him.

Tiptoe Tortoise off the side of the stage.

Put the moon prop up above the hare's head. Start making 'waking up' noises (yawns and snuffles) and then quickly straighten up the hare puppet.

Hare

Goodness me. It's nighttime! I must have slept for ages. I'd better get on and finish the race.

Hare dashes off one side of the stage.
Take the moon off.

Hold the tortoise up together with the finish flag.

Tortoise: Here's the finish line. Most of the crowd seems to have gone home. Never mind.

Tortoise moves across the stage, passing the flag.

Tortoise: Hurrah. I've won!

Take off the tortoise and hold up the hare, who rushes across the stage, passing the flag.

Hare

> I can't believe it! I lost to a trundling old tortoise. The shame of it. How will I ever explain it to my friends?

Take off the flag. Bring on the tortoise and the hare together.

Tortoise

Tell them you've learnt a new lesson.
It's no good rushing if you don't do a good job.

Pop your head up between your puppets.

Puppeteer

Who do you think did the good job today ...
the tortoise or the hare?

Wait for the audience to reply.

Puppeteer

And don't forget me. Goodbye!

THE END